Yummy Food
...that's good for you!

Yummy Food

...that's good for you!

WENDY HOOD

MY H.E.A.L.T.H.
KICK

Helping Everyone Achieve Life Through Healthy Habits™

www.myhealthkick.com

Layout Design - Pam Rose
Photos - Yazmin Wickham, Wendy Hood, Pam Rose
Editing - Hazel Metcalf, Joyce Mullins

DEDICATION

This book is dedicated to all who want to take back the ownership of what they are eating and what they are feeding their families. People who desire to live vibrant and energetic lives. People who want to eat well without sacrificing the taste of the food. People who want to get back to good eating, good nutritional value foods and people who want to rid their bodies of the toxins that pollute a lot of the foods today. Lastly to people who want to be proactive in their health. Enjoy!

Table of Contents

Tips

FOREWARD

My daughter, Wendy Hood, has always amazed me with her movement in the kitchen since way back…creating meals that were so beyond a 12 or 13 year old. Back then it was homemade French fries, so good from scratch; the best mashed potatoes that you could ever imagine; hamburgers that had seasoning from another planet and made to order for each family member or whoever happened to be present.

We normally shopped every Saturday for groceries, and along about Wednesday I would wonder where my groceries were disappearing to. Years later I learned that my kitchen would turn into a neighborhood eatery for breakfast and lunch. Wendy would take orders and prepare the food and all the neighborhood kids would show up.

So here we are years later with a cookbook that is jammed full of healthy recipes and wonderful cooking tips created by Wendy who has dedicated her life to healthy eating and healthy living. This is a book chalked full of healthy YUMMY FOR THE TUMMY recipes.

I always knew that she would put a cookbook out…that was a childhood dream…who said dreams don't come true?

Alverrene Bridgeforth

ACKNOWLEDGMENTS

There are many people that I wish to thank who have contributed to the production of this cook book. First, I would like to thank my Mother who taught me to cook. We were expected to help in the kitchen, and for me it no longer became a chore but a … "looking forward to experience!" My siblings, Missy (Michelle), Michael, and Stephanie, were always so happy to get a break from cooking because I loved it so much. Missy, Stephanie, and Michael made me believe at a young age that I could cook anything that I wanted to without a recipe and it was delicious. I can hear my brother now… "Wendy, can you make me some more…?" My dad was another incredible encourager! He was the "taster." I always had to get Daddy's approval. If my dad liked it, that's all that mattered. I remember the holidays when my dad would be carving the bird, and say, "Pssst…Wendy, come here." I would run to him and he would sneak me a piece of turkey or standing rib roast. It was our 'Yummy'! We were the tasters! That's how I learned that you've gotta taste it before you eat it.

God has placed beautiful people in my life today that have ignited me to execute what has been simmering since I was 14. Thank you to Hazel Metcalf and Pam Rose for your continued encouragement and support. Your willingness to help me has touched me and I thank you more than you can imagine.

Dennis, my incredible loving husband, encourages me daily. I think he knew if he married me, he would eat well. Today when we have dinner, he says, "Why would we ever go out to eat, when we can eat like this at home?" My kids, Tyler, Tori, and Taryn, can all cook. They all love to eat, too! Out of the three of them Taryn likes to cook the most. Tyler is our birthday cake man and Tori can cook it all but would rather just eat what I prepare. They fill me up with encouragement as well.

I am extremely grateful to GOD for the opportunity to share recipes in this cookbook. It is all of His work and to Him be the glory. I thank our LORD and Savior for the gift of taste, for the wonderful herbs that He created, and for the vibrant vegetables and fruit that were created for our enjoyment. Thank you LORD for the people you have put into my life to encourage me along the way.

Let's Get Started

Make the healthiest choices for your family.

Most people want to eat healthy but feel that they can't afford it. A lot of my clients say buying organic is too expensive. Research has shown that it can cost as much as 50% more — so buy it only when it's worth it.

What is organic food, anyway?

Organic food must adhere to specific standards regulated by the United States Department of Agriculture (USDA). Crops are generally grown without synthetic pesticides, artificial fertilizers, irradiation (a form of radiation used to kill bacteria), or biotechnology. Animals on organic farms eat organically grown feed, aren't confined 100 percent of the time (as they sometimes are on conventional farms), and are raised without antibiotics or synthetic growth hormones.

Is organic food better for me?

Organic foods may have higher nutritional value than conventional food, according to some research. The reason: In the absence of pesticides and fertilizers, plants boost their production of the phytochemicals (vitamins and antioxidants) that strengthen their resistance to bugs and weeds. Some studies have linked pesticides in our food to everything from headaches to cancer to birth defects — but many experts maintain that the levels in conventional food are safe for most healthy adults. Even low-level pesticide exposure, however, can be significantly more toxic for fetuses and children (due to their less-developed immune systems) and for pregnant women (it puts added strain on their already taxed organs), according to research.

Pesticide contamination isn't as much of a concern in meats and dairy products (animals may consume some pesticides, depending on their diet), but many scientists are concerned about the antibiotics being given to most farm animals. Many are the same antibiotics humans rely on, and overuse of these drugs has already enabled bacteria to develop resistance to them, rendering them less effective in fighting infection, says a nonprofit research organization.

Is buying organic better for the environment?
Organic farming reduces pollutants in groundwater and creates richer soil that aids plant growth while reducing erosion. It also decreases pesticides that can end up in your drinking glass; in some cities, pesticides in tap water have been measured at unsafe levels for weeks at a time.

When is it worth the splurge?
If you can afford it, buy local and organic. Farmers' markets carry reasonably priced locally grown organic and conventional food; to find one in your area, go to localharvest.org. If you can't always afford organic, do spend the extra money when it comes to the "dirty dozen": peaches, strawberries, nectarines, apples, spinach, celery, pears, sweet bell peppers, cherries, potatoes, lettuce, and imported grapes. These fragile fruits and vegetables often require more pesticides to fight off bugs compared to hardier produce, such as asparagus and broccoli.

My personal source for organic fruits and veggies is localfoodstop.com. This is only for my area; however, if you go to local harvest.org you can find your local provider. Another inexpensive way to get organic fruits and vegetable is to grow them yourself. It can be done. If I can do it, so can you. Start small and reap a harvest of goodies!

When shopping for organic foods, always look for the USDA seal on any kind of packaged food. For meat and dairy, this seal ensures you're getting antibiotic- and hormone-free products. When buying meat or produce that isn't packaged, look for a sign stating that it's organic, or ask the store clerk.

About the Cookbook

This cook book, *Yummy Food ... that's good for you,* gives you family sized recipes. If you are cooking for one or two people you will need to adjust accordingly. We hope you are inspired to get into your kitchen and create meals that you and your family will enjoy for generations to come. This cook book is full of information that will not only help you make new meals but provide you with information to help you achieve life through healthy habits. That is what our company, "My H.E.A.L.T.H. Kick,"™ stands for.

If one is motivated, they could use this *Yummy Food* cookbook as a start to a new YOU. It is comprised of recipes that are categorized into three sections: Phase 1 ❶, Phase 2 ❷, or Phase 3 ❸. If my plan were to "get healthier," "to burn fat," or to change the uncontrollable sweet or salt cravings, I would stick to only Phase 1 recipes for 6 weeks, then I would move to enjoying phase 1 and Phase 2 recipes for 6 weeks. After assessing my weight loss and inch loss, I would move on the Phase 3 category where you can enjoy foods from all three categories.

The purpose of Phase 1 is to rid your body of unwanted "toxins" that have built up over the years. Recipes in this phase are filled with antioxidant enriching foods.

If there is not a need for weight loss, you just truly desire healthy foods, then you have purchased the right book. Enjoy it all, eat clean, be vibrant, and enjoy your energy!

In this Yummy Foods, you will not find:
> Artificial Sweeteners
> Artificial Flavors and Colors
> Corn Syrup
> Imitation Meat Products
> Shellfish
> Soft Drinks
> Pork Products
> White Flour (or)
> White Sugar

I encourage all of my clients to shop organic when they can, eat meals that are low-glycemic, to drink plenty of water, and exercise regularly. I like to kickbox – *the official way to knock the stress out of your life.*

Lastly, before we jump into the recipes, remember these things:

- Buy organic, hormone free when possible
- Wild freshwater/ocean caught fish is best
- Chicken and turkey – free range and organic is best
- Lunch meat – organic and hormone free
- Dairy (very limited amounts, hormone free, organic)
- Eggs – cage free/omega 3/organic
- Oils at high heat – extra virgin coconut oil and hormone free, organic butter
- Oils best after cooking or cold –
  - Extra virgin olive oil
  - Flax seed oil
  - Expeller pressed sesame oil
  - Expeller pressed peanut oil
- Sweetners
  - Raw honey, or locally grown
  - Real maple syrup
  - Organic succanat
- Beverages
  - Purified – non chlorinated water
  - Natural sparkling water
  - Herbal teas
  - Raw vegetable juice (juiced in your own juicer)
  - Certified organic coffee

This is how you eat clean, toxin-free foods that make you feel FANTASTIC!

As with any healthy eating or exercise plan, you should consult your physician before beginning or changing your eating or exercise plan.

DIRTY DOZEN	CLEANEST 12
Buy these organic	Lowest in pesticides
Peaches	Onions
Apples	Avocado
Sweet Bell Peppers	Sweet Corn (Frozen)
Celery	Pineapples
Nectarines	Mango
Strawberries	Sweet Peas (Frozen)
Cherries	Asparagus
Lettuce	Kiwi
Grapes (Imported)	Bananas
Pears	Cabbage
Spinach	Broccoli
Potatoes	Eggplant

Breakfast

Many people skip breakfast. They are rushed, don't have the time, not hungry, and the list goes on. Have you ever heard someone say that breakfast is the most important meal of the day? They were right. Eating breakfast gets your metabolism started and gives to the energy needed to get through the day. Start your day with breakfast. Some people become too rushed and just eat a donut with a cup of coffee, or a commercial boxed juice drink. The healthiest thing for you to do is to eat a low-glycemic balanced meal that will provide you with energy that is necessary to study well or to perform well at work.

I am always impressed when it is testing time at school and I receive a recorded message or a note from the school that indicates, "Your child should eat a well-balanced breakfast so they do well on the test." What is well-balanced? Well, the sugary cereals are out. They will spike your blood sugar and provide no nutritional value. I'm speaking of the most popular advertised ones here. A better idea is to eat fruits, consider steel cut oatmeal, homemade breakfast bars, Greek yogurt, omega-3 cage-free organic eggs, and it's not too early to throw in some veggies. Have fun with it. It's the beginning of your day. You deserve to feel vibrant, energetic, and ready to rip!

Smoothies: A key ingredient to a yummy smoothie is a good natural extract. Please visit www.myhealthkick.com for a full recommendation on where they are available.

Veggie Omelet

2 eggs
Coconut oil
Bell peppers (finely diced)
8-10 leaves of fresh spinach
5 cherry tomatoes (cut in half lengthwise)
Raw feta cheese
Sea salt
Pepper to taste

Add just enough coconut oil to the heavy skillet to oil the pan. Beat 2 eggs, and add a pinch of sea salt and pepper. Pour the eggs into a medium-hot skillet. As eggs begin to cook use your spatula to slightly bring the eggs to the center from all sides. Tip uncooked eggs to the sides. Add tomatoes, spinach, cheese, and green bell pepper to one side of your egg mixture. Get ready for the flip! Loosen the egg around the sides of the pan, so when you flip it, it all folds over easily. Here we go… FLIP (Fold) one side of the egg on top to create a "½ sandwich." After about 30 sec, flip the entire omelet over. Add a pinch of Celtic sea salt and pepper to the top of you omelet. ❶

Scrambled Eggs

2 scrambled eggs to your liking with sea salt and pepper. Serve with a slice of turkey bacon.

Variation – add ⅛ cup mozzarella cheese, and ½ tsp of fresh parsley to the scrambled egg mixture for cheesy eggs.

Oil a heavy pan with coconut oil. Heat the pan while you are whisking the egg mixture. Pour the egg mixture in the pan and let them sit for a second, scramble the eggs and let them sit for a few more seconds. Take off of the heat while cooking so you do not overcook your eggs as they will continue to cook off of the heat. ❶

Steel Cut Oatmeal

Why steel cut vs. instant? The steel-cut oats are whole grain oats and have a lower glycemic index than instant oats. In other words they are slowly digested and gradually released as sugar into the bloodstream.

Research shows that eating oats, oat bran, and oatmeal helps lower elevated blood cholesterol level thanks to their special type of soluble fibre. This soluble fibre also helps stabilize blood sugar levels by reducing spikes and dips, especially in people with type 2 diabetes.

These little friends are a great source of vitamin B1 (thiamin), vitamin B2 (riboflavin), and vitamin E.

Here's where we go wrong: Using the instant or quick oatmeal and adding sugar. Feel free to add your berries, a little bit of raw honey, or cinnamon to your oatmeal for sweetness if you would like. ❶

Berries

Strawberries
Blackberries
Blue berries

Rinse and prepare your fruit. I like to cut my strawberries in ½ lengthwise. These are high in anti-oxidants and will provide you with the perfect boost, not to mention a healthy snack. By all means, DO NOT add any sugar. God has supplied all of your needs right here in these healthy sweet fruits. ❶

Turkey Sausage

1 lb ground turkey
2 tsp garlic
1 ½ crushed fennel seed
1 tsp salt
1 tsp dried oregano
1 tsp dried sage

Mix it all together and shape into turkey patties. Refrigerate for 8 hours or overnight. ❶

Strawberry - Lemonade Smoothie

2 cups of water
1 cup of frozen strawberries
½ to 1 cup ice chips
1 Tbsp lemon juice
6 oz. vanilla Greek yogurt
   or 15 grams protein 100% Isolate powder

Combine these ingredients in a blender. ❶

Strawberry or Blueberry Cheesecake Smoothie

1 oz. fat free organic cream cheese
2 cups frozen strawberries or blueberries
1 ½ cup water
1 tsp Stevia
6 oz. vanilla Greek yogurt
   or 15 grams protein 100% Isolate powder

Combine these ingredients in a blender. ❷

Orange Cream Smoothie

½ - ¾ cup ice chips
1 cup water
½ tsp orange extract
6 oz. vanilla Greek yogurt
   or 15 grams protein 100% Isolate powder

Combine these ingredients in a blender. ❶

Banana Blast Smoothie

1 ½ cups of water
¾ to 1 cup ice chips
½ tsp banana extract
½ peeled and frozen banana
6 oz. vanilla Greek yogurt
   or 15 grams protein 100% Isolate powder

Combine these ingredients in a blender. ❶

Berry Time Smoothie

½ cup frozen mixed berries
½ cup ice
10 oz. Water
6 oz. vanilla Greek yogurt
  or 15 grams protein 100% Isolate powder

Combine these ingredients in a blender. ❶

Morning Coffee Smoothie

10-12 cubes of frozen organic coffee
½ tsp vanilla extract
1 tsp raw honey
¾ cup Greek vanilla yogurt
  or 15 grams protein 100% Isolate powder

Brew a slightly stronger than normal pot of organic coffee, pour into ice trays and place into the freezer. When frozen, add all of the ingredients together and Yummy morning! ❶

Mocha Smoothie

Same as above, just add 2 Tbsp cocoa powder ❷

Mint Chocolate Shake

1 cup water
1 tsp mint extract
1 cup ice
1 Tbsp cocoa powder
6 oz. vanilla Greek yogurt
  or 15 grams protein 100% Isolate powder

Combine these ingredients in a blender. ❷

Note: Most blenders have a smoothie setting; make sure that you use that setting and blend until you reach your desired consistency.

Pumpkin Smoothie

10 oz. water
½ cup canned pumpkin
¼ tsp cinnamon
⅛ tsp nutmeg
1 tsp raw honey
½ cup ice cubes
¾ cup Greek yogurt
  or 15 grams protein 100% Isolate powder

Combine these ingredients in a blender. You can top this with a ½ scoop of yogurt and some cinnamon sprinkles. ❷

Root Beer Float Smoothie

10 oz. water
½ cup ice
1 ½ tsp root beer extract
6 oz. vanilla Greek yogurt
  or 15 grams protein 100% Isolate powder

Combine these ingredients in a blender.   ❶

Tropical Sunrise Smoothie

10 oz. water
½ cup ice
½ cup frozen tropical fruit (pineapple, mango)
6 oz. vanilla Greek yogurt

Combine these ingredients in a blender.   ❷

The Benefits of Water

Almost everyone knows that you should drink 8-10 glasses of water a day. But do you really think that it is necessary?

Yes it is! Let me tell you why. Almost every cell in your body needs water to function properly. Our bodies which are made up of 55 and 75 percent water (lean people have more water in their bodies because muscle holds more water than fat), are in need of consistent water replenishment.

Your lungs expel between two and four cups of water each day through normal breathing – even more on a cold day. If your feet sweat, there goes another cup of water. If you make many trips to the bathroom during the day, there goes more water; if you perspire, you expel water (which doesn't include exercise induced perspiration).

You would need to lose about 10 percent of your body weight in fluids to be considered dehydrated, but as little as 2 percent can affect athletic performance, cause tiredness, or affect thinking abilities. I encourage all of my clients to drink one half of their body weight in ounces of water per day.

Water is the miracle drink that will do wonders for your health.

If you don't like it, please learn to. I've got some great ideas for you to help you out!!

Salads

What a fun way to get veggies down. But eaters beware here! Did you know that salads could also become unhealthy? Oh yeah. Once you start loading the unnecessary toppings and fat filled dressings, you might as well go and get a double bacon burger with all the toppings because the fat content could be close to the same. The idea of a salad is to eat clean crisp raw vegetables with fun tasty toppings that provide maximum nutrients and leave you feeling clean and fresh. Watch out for fast food restaurants that sweeten their salads and/or salad dressings to make them addictive. Know what you are eating, and if it is a salad, make sure it does what you are looking for.

Dressings to accompany these salads can be found on page 86-87 of this Yummy Cookbook!!

Umm! Yummy, yummy fresh!

Small Green Salad

8 oz. bag of spring mix greens
2-3 roma tomatoes
2 shredded carrots
1 diced bell pepper (any color)
Vegetables - choose 2 more (mushrooms, onions, avocado)

Toss together and then drizzle with Balsamic Vinaigrette Dressing. ❶

Chef Salad

8 oz. green leafy mix
2-3 boiled eggs
2-3 florets of broccoli
2 carrots, shredded
1 red and green peppers
½ small onion
4 oz. of diced turkey

Toss vegetables together and add Ranch Dressing. ❷

Italian Salad

Romaine lettuce
Fresh baby spinach
1 handful of cherry tomatoes
1 handful of kalamata olives
5-6 slices of salami quartered (not pork)
¼ fresh red onion sliced thinly
Toasted pine nuts
Fresh parmesan cheese.

Mix well and add Italian Dressing. ❶

Bright Veggie Salad

2 carrots
1 pepper
3-4 mushrooms
3-4 florets of broccoli
½ cucumber
2 tomatoes

Toss with a vinaigrette dressing of your choice. ❶

Easy Vegetable Salad

1 head romaine, boston, or red leaf lettuce
½ zucchini, quartered
½ cucumber, quartered
2 plum tomatoes chopped
½ red onion, sliced
2-3 oz. raw cheddar cheese, grated
Dressing of your choice

Place enough lettuce to cover the bottom of your salad bowl, then add a layer each of the other items, then another layer of lettuce repeating until all ingredients are used up. Serve the dressing on the side or mix into the entire salad and serve. ❶

Waldorf Salad

¼ cup mayonnaise (page 89)
¼ cup plain Greek yogurt
1 Tbsp lemon juice
1 tsp fat free skim milk
2 medium red apples coarsely chopped (2 cups)
2 medium celery stalks, chopped (1 cup)
2 Tbsp coarsely chopped nuts
Salad greens.

Mix the mayonnaise, yogurt, lemon juice and milk together. Stir in the apples, celery and nuts. Serve over salad greens. ❷

Greek Salad

Romaine lettuce
1 chopped cucumber
1 chopped tomato
½ cup red onion
½ cup organic feta cheese
3 tsp fresh oregano leaves (sliced)
Lemon juice and olive oil dressing

Combine all ingredients and mix with the Lemon Juice Dressing! ❶

Mixed Greens and Fruit Salad

Use the mixture of greens you prefer for a base. Add as many veggies as you can such as broccoli, carrots, peppers, mushrooms, tomatoes, cucumbers, then add strawberry slices as well as almond slivers. ❶

Spinach, Walnut & Strawberry Salad

Spinach leaves
Strawberries
Walnuts
Feta cheese

Top a bed of Spinach leaves with a handful of sliced strawberries, walnuts, and feta cheese. Make a Red Wine Vinaigrette Dressing: olive oil and red wine vinegar, add dried parsley, and just a dab of Dijon mustard. ❶

Asian Chicken Salad

3 grilled chicken breasts
Bibb lettuce
3-4 lemon balm leaves
Peapods
Thinly sliced carrots
Thinly sliced red bell peppers
½ cup mandarin orange slices (packed in juice)
Raw slivered almonds - as a topping
Sesame Dressing (page 88)
Sea salt
Pepper
Sesame seeds

Season the chicken breast with sea salt and pepper. Place into a heated electric grill oiled with a little sesame oil. As your chicken is grilling, pour the juice from the mandarin oranges on top of the chicken. Cut the lemon balm leaves and let it fall onto the chicken. Slice it as it is cooking and then take out.

Prepare the Bibb lettuce on plates, and then add the rest of the toppings. Put the chicken on last and drizzle with dressing, then top with a few more sesame seeds. YUMOLA! FRESH!! ❶

Tuna Salad

3 cans of tuna in water
½ cup mayonnaise (page 89)
2 Tbsp mustard
¼ cup finely chopped small onion
¼ cup celery
2 Tbsp dill pickle relish
3 hardboiled eggs

Mix it all together and add a little sea salt and pepper to taste. Serve on a bed of green leaf lettuce. Add or delete ingredients based on your preference. ❶

* For Phase 2 you may have it on Ezekiel Bread ❷

* For Phase 3 you may have it on whole grain bread, whole wheat sour dough, or a healthy variety of your choice. ❸

Chicken Salad

2 cups cooked cubed chicken
⅓ cup grated carrots
½ cups quartered red seedless grapes
2 tsp lemon juice
⅓ cup mayonnaise (page 89)
Sea salt
Pepper
Finely chopped celery
Onion

Mix up all ingredients and sever on a bed of green leaf lettuce. Add or delete ingredients based on your preference. ❶

* For Phase 2 you may have it on Ezekiel Bread ❷

* For Phase 3 you may have it on whole grain bread, whole wheat sour dough, or a healthy variety of your choice. ❸

Toasted Almond Chicken Salad

3 skinless chicken breasts
1 – 15 oz. can of organic chicken broth
1 Tbsp fresh tarragon, chopped
3 Tbsp almond slivers, toasted
¼ cup organic mayonnaise
2 Tbsp plain fat-free yogurt
½ tsp sea salt
Black pepper
1 6-9 oz. salad greens

Place chicken breasts in a large saucepan over medium heat. Pour chicken broth over chicken breasts and bring to a low simmer for 20 minutes or until done. Shred chicken meat and set aside to cool. In a medium bowl, combine remaining ingredients, except salad greens, and mix well. Mix the chicken and toss well to coat. Place your chicken mixture on a bed of dark green leafy greens. ❷

Corn and Bean Salad

½ bag of frozen organic sweet corn
2 cans fire roasted diced tomatoes drained
½ can black beans, drained and rinsed
¼ cup chopped red onion
3 tsp chopped fresh cilantro
2 Tbsp fresh lime juice
1 Tbsp olive oil
sea salt
½ tsp ground cumin
¼ tsp pepper
1 clove garlic, finely chopped
1 avocado chopped

Cook the corn as directed and rinse with cold water. Stir together all of the remaining ingredients except avocado. When you are ready to serve, add the avocado. Place on salad greens with cooked diced chicken. You will have left overs…Yay! ❷

Tex-Mex Salad

Red or green romaine lettuce
Organic frozen cooked corn (rinsed and cooled)
1 15-oz. can cooked black beans (rinsed and cooled)
Salsa – for a topping
2 diced roma tomatoes
1 diced alvocado
Crushed organic blue corn chips

Spread your lettuce mixture on your plate. Add corn, black beans, salsa, extra roma tomatoes, avocado, and a few pieces of Lays Blue Corn Chips. They are the NATURAL ONES. Crunch about 4 chips in your fist and add to the top of your salad. Use Organic Ranch, page 89, 2 Tbsp only. ❷

Sesame Steak Salad

Ahhhh!! I just finished eating this, so this is how I made it!!! YUMMY!! Flavor-ish-ous!

1 lb thinly sliced flank steak
Red leaf lettuce
2 red tomatoes (sliced)
½ cup fresh broccoli
1 handful of snow pea pods
½ cup grated carrots
¼ cup of red onions
Sesame seeds
Sesame Dressing (page 88)

Place the sliced steak in your electric frying pan on low heat, no oil needed just let it warm and create its own juices. Sprinkle some sea salt and pepper to taste. Flip, repeat. You should season on both sides. After it's brown, but you can tell it's still pink inside, add sesame oil to the top and keep it on low, flip and repeat to the other side. Cook it to your liking…I like it medium. Prepare your salad plates. Start with the lettuce, add the veggies, sprinkle with sesame seeds and add your homemade Asian Sesame Dressing! YUUMMMM! YIPPEE! ❶

Yummy Fruit Salad

1 pineapple
1 Macintosh apple
1 ½ limes
1 banana
1 red papaya
1 cup pecans
Red grapes (seedless)

Quarter the Pineapple. Cut the pineapple away from the husk, saving the quartered husk with the stem attached. Cut the pineapple, apple, banana, and the papaya into cubes. Add the grapes and the pecans. Mix together in a bowl being careful not to mash the bananas. Squeeze the juice of the lime on the diced fruit. Now you are ready to use your husks that you've set aside as a serving dish. Rinse the husks and pat the outsides of them dry with a paper towel. Line them up on a fruit platter, all facing the same direction. Scoop the fruit on to the quartered pineapple shells. Quarter the remaining lime and decorate for garnish. YUMMY! Not only is this a refreshing fruit salad, it is a beautiful presentation! ❷

5 Reasons to Switch to Water

Helps to keep headaches away: Three quarters of your brain is water. This is one of the first places that we will feel it when we are not drinking enough water

Reduces Infections: The lymphatic system is your waste disposal system, breaking down toxins like caffeine before passing them into the blood stream. Dehydration weakens the flow of lymph in the system and makes the body less resistant to infection. With water lymph flows properly again, fighting infection and lowering feverish temperatures.

Gives you better skin: Skin needs to be hydrated, if you are only consuming a little bit of water your skin will be dry. Also removes dark circles around the eyes. Skin is bruised if not hydrated enough.

Keeps up your concentration: Your body needs water to help flush out poisons from things like junk food and additives. If you are dehydrated, toxins from the junk food stay in the liver, making you tired and unable to concentrate. Water moves the poisons out and gets the system moving again.

Stops Cramps: Blood transports oxygen to the muscles for activities such as exercise. If there isn't enough oxygen in the blood, the muscles create lactic acid which causes painful cramps. Drinking more water helps to keep blood pumped with oxygen.

Tasty Waters

Crisp Minty Lemon Water
Water
Lemon wedge
2-3 leaves of mint (bruise the leaf to get the flavor)
Ice

Strawberry Water
Water
2-3 frozen strawberries
Ice

Fresh Water
A slice of cucumber with the skin
A twist of lime

Tropical Water
4 or 5 pieces of tropical frozen fruit
Water
Ice

All of these recipes are great alternatives to soda! Say no to the SODA POP!! (My middle name use to be Soda Pop Girl.)

When choosing water, make spring water your first choice and purified water your second choice.

Wraps

Wraps are a very YUMMY way to throw down on a sandwich without the extra fat of bread. Use whole grain sprouted wraps instead of a white flour tortilla. They are healthy, satisfying, and delicious. Wraps can be cold or hot and they are the perfect portion for lunch. Accompany a wrap with a side of fruit and a refreshing Crisp Minty Lemon Water and you will have enjoyed a great meal!

Turkey and Goat Cheese Wrap

Turkey slices (free of nitrates)
6-8 whole wheat wraps
2 diced roma tomatoes
6 oz. bag of spinach leaves
½ cup crumbled raw feta cheese
1 julienned cut cucumber
Balsamic Vinaigrette Dressing

Place a few slices of turkey on a spouted whole wheat wrap and layer with spinach leaves, tomatoes, cucumbers, Balsamic Vinaigrette Dressing, and feta cheese. Yum! ❷

Grrrlll—(I am rolling my rr's growling…this is Yummy)!

Southwestern Chicken Wrap

3 boneless, skinless chicken breasts
Juice from 1 lime
Sea salt
Pepper
2 cloves of garlic, crushed
Chili powder
2 cups cooked Basmati rice
1 15oz. can black beans
3 Tbsp salsa
6-8 whole grain wraps
⅛ cup cilantro
2 diced roma tomatoes
Chipotle Sauce (page 90)

Using an electric skillet, grill your chicken in the lime juice. Season it while cooking. Add sea salt, pepper, Chili powder, diced tomatoes, and fresh garlic. Slice the chicken as it is cooking until you dice it in several pieces. In a small sauce pan, heat the black beans until warm; add a few pinches of the cilantro, and the salsa. Stir and simmer for 5 minutes.

Fill the center of each wrap with the chicken mixture, the black bean mixture and a spoonful of Basmati rice. Top with a little cilantro, some chipotle sauce and tightly roll your wrap. I like to cut mine in a diagonal. Supper YUMMY!!! ❸

Buffalo Chicken Wrap

3 chicken breasts
Sea salt
Pepper
2 Tbsp coconut oil
2 diced tomatoes
6 oz. bag of fresh spinach
Small slice of Monterey Jack cheese
Ranch Dressing (page 89)
6-8 sprouted whole grain wraps
Buffalo Sauce (page 90)

Put the oil in a medium skillet; when warm, add the chicken breast. Sprinkle the salt and pepper on each side. Cook the chicken until done, about 4-6 minutes on each side. Cut the chicken into cubes. Put it back into the pan and cover it with Buffalo Sauce. Simmer the little cubes for about 5 minutes covered. Pull out 6-8 whole grain wraps and place a little bit of Ranch Dressing on the bottom of each wrap. Then add the Monterey Jack cheese, then a spoon full of the chunky hot chicken, next lettuce and tomatoes. Drizzle a little more buffalo sauce over the tomatoes. Tightly wrap and cut on a diagonal. THIS IS MY HUSBAND'S FAVORITE WRAP! THE MANLY WRAP! ❸

Skinny Turkey Wrap

Turkey slices (free of nitrates)
Celery or green onions
Organic cream cheese

Take your turkey slice and with a knife, spread the cream cheese directly on the meat. Add your cut and cleaned celery or green onion or both and roll it up tightly, like a log. What a great snack!! YUM!! ❶

Naked Chicken Burrito

3 chicken breast
1 Tbsp chile powder
1 tsp onion powder
Sea salt
Pepper
6 oz. mixed salad greens
2 roma tomatoes
½ small onions, diced
Cooked black beans
Guacamole (page 93)
Sour cream (as a topping)
Salsa (as a topping)

Season cooked chicken with chile powder, garlic powder, onion powder, sea salt, and pepper. Add about ⅓ cup of water and simmer for about 15 minutes. On a plate, place greens, tomatoes, onions, guacamole, sour cream, salsa, cooked black beans, and then top with your seasoned chicken. ❶

Burritos

1 lb ground turkey
Sea salt
Pepper
1 cup Enchilada Sauce (page 90)
1 15-oz. can of black beans
3 Tbsp of salsa

Toppings:
2 diced roma tomatoes
Fresh spinach leaves
1 cup of raw cheddar cheese
Organic sour cream (optional topping)
Salsa (optional topping)
Cilantro (optional topping)
Diced onions (optional topping)
Whole grain sprouted tortillas
  (or) spinach tortillas

In a skillet brown the ground turkey, adding sea salt and pepper while cooking. When the meat is cooked thoroughly, add the enchilada sauce, black beans, and salsa. Simmer for about 15 minutes. Taste it. Does it pass the taste test? Ummm! On a griddle, heat each tortilla, flip it, and load it with desired ingredients. Make it to order, they're gonna love it! Yummy way to enjoy a burrito without all of the fat, hydrogenated oils, and stuff that's not so good for you! Make it at home....'Ole! ❷

Sides & Pastas

In order to feel as though a meal is complete, you want to pair it with side dishes. This is typically where the meal goes wrong. Choose vegetable dishes as sides. Watch the high-glycemic carbohydrates as they are the culprits, they are known as the "comfort foods." They make you feel good temporarily, but not in the long run. Are they really comforting? Something that harms you and causes your blood sugar to rise isn't very comforting.

Choose clean fresh ingredients. Stay away from the boxed processed items that are filled with preservatives and artificial ingredients.

If you are eating out, ask your server for healthy choices. Good restaurants always have choices for those with healthier eating goals.

Enjoy!

Raw Vegetables

Carrots
Red bell peppers
Yellow bell peppers
Orange bell peppers
Beefy tomatoes
Onions

Wash and prepare all of your Veggies for cutting! Peel the carrots. Slice them at an angle, in thin slices. (Not too thin, but not thick), you want these to be easy to eat. Next cut the tops off of the bell peppers rinsing out all of the seeds. Cut these into long thing strips. Cut the stem off the tomatoes and cut these in thin wedges. Cut the onion into thinly sliced rings. Place these veggies on a platter, grouping them by color. If you have a meat dish with them, place them around the edges of the platter with the meat in the center. I would recommend pairing this dish with Pineapple Chicken, page 56. ❶

Spinach

Spinach
Garlic
Almonds

Sauté spinach with fresh garlic and almonds in a lightly oiled pan (coconut oil). ❶

Red Parmesan Potatoes

8-10 small red potatoes
1 clove of garlic, crushed
Sea salt to taste
Pepper to taste
1 cup of potato broth
½ cup of organic milk
1 cup parmesan cheese
1 tsp fresh parsley

Clean and cut the red potatoes into chunks, leaving the skin on. Boil them on high heat until tender along with the garlic. When the little reds break apart easily, drain them, reserving 1 cup of the potato broth. Put them back into the pan and add sea salt and pepper. Slightly mash the potatoes with a fork and then add back in about ¼ of the broth. Stir, then add ½ of the milk and stir. Continue to add the liquids until you have reached the desired consistency. Stir in the cheese and the parsley. I like my potatoes to have a little chunky surprise here and there. Yuuummmmm! ❸

Oven Baked Garlic Red Potatoes

8–10 small red potatoes
4–5 cloves of garlic, crushed
3 tsp organic butter
Sea salt
2 tsp parsley
Pepper

Rinse, clean, and pat dry the potatoes. Chunk them a little larger then dicing. Rub a glass dish with coconut oil and place the potatoes inside. Flavor the potatoes with sea salt, pepper, and add the parsley. Evenly distribute the garlic on top of the potatoes and then add the butter to the top the potatoes. Bake at 400°F for about 30 minutes, or until the potatoes are soft and a fork easily pierces the potatoes. ❸

Steamed Broccoli with Toasted Almonds

½ cup of raw almonds
2 bunches of broccoli
Sea salt to taste
Pepper to taste

Take the raw almonds and spread them evenly on a cookie sheet. Bake in a pre-heated oven at 400° for 15 minutes. While the almonds are baking, prepare a double boiler on top of the stove. When the water comes to a boil, add the cut and cleaned broccoli to the top. Use a lid for quick cooking. I like my broccoli just barely cooked so I get all of the yummy nutrients from it. Add a little sea salt and pepper. When it is finished, take it off of the eye and add the slivered almonds to it. Yummmm, Crunch away! ❶

Tri-Color Veggies

4 large carrots
3 summer squash
3 zucchini
1 tsp dill
1 Tbsp butter
2 Tbsp filtered water

Pre-heat oven to 350°. Clean, peel and dry the carrots. Clean the squash and zucchini. I have a wavy cutter and I love the way it looks with these veggies. Cut them all on a diagonal and place in a 3-quart buttered glass dish. Layer them by color and sprinkle the dill on top. Add the butter to a few places on top and then drizzle the water over the veggies. Bake at 350° for 20 minutes or until desired tenderness. ❶

Roasted Asparagus

1 lb asparagus spears (thick spears are best for roasting)
2 Tbsp organic butter
Juice of 1 lemon
2 cloves garlic, minced
Sea salt
Freshly grated black pepper
1 tsp fresh parsley

Preheat the oven to 400°. Wash and cut the ends of the asparagus at an angle. In a sauce pan, combine the butter, lemon juice, and the garlic. Heat until the butter is melted. Line the asparagus in a 13x9 glass baking dish. Pour the butter mixture over the asparagus. With a fork, roll the asparagus back and forth until it is covered with the butter mixture. Sprinkle with sea salt and pepper. Bake the asparagus in the oven for 8-10 minutes, or until when pierced with a fork it is tender. Squeeze more lemon juice over the asparagus and sprinkle the fresh parsley over the top before serving. ❶

Honey Glazed Carrots

1 lb carrots, peeled
2-3 Tbsp organic butter
1 tsp sea salt
⅓ cup vegetable broth
2 Tbsp raw honey
¼ teaspoon white pepper (optional)

Slice the carrots into diagonally. Try to cut the pieces so they are about the same size as each other so they cook evenly. Melt the butter in a sauce pan over medium-high heat and add the carrots. Toss to combine and reduce the heat to medium. Sprinkle the salt over carrots and toss again. Sauté for 3-4 minutes, then add the raw honey and white pepper and toss to combine. Add the broth. Cover the pot and cook for another 3 minutes. I like them crispy-tender, not tender-tender. Uncover the pot and increase heat to medium-high. Toss the carrots around again, and cook away most of the liquid. Turn off the heat and taste. Is it Yummy? ❶

Sweet Potatoes

3-4 sweet potatoes
2 Tbsp organic butter
2 Tbsp raw honey
2 tsp cinnamon

Clean 3-4 large sweet potatoes and pat dry. Lightly oil a glass baking dish. Peel and slice the potatoes (the short way, like potato chips but thicker) and lay them in a glass baking pan. Add a few slices of butter on the sweet potatoes and sprinkle cinnamon. Cook until the potatoes are tender, about 30 minutes. ❸

Pasta Salad

1 14.5-oz. box of penne pasta whole grain
1 bag of pre-washed/cut broccoli slaw with snow peas
Balsamic Vinaigrette Dressing
Sea salt
Pepper

Prepare the whole grain pasta according to the package directions. Rinse with cold water. Add the vegetable mix, the dressing, and add in salt and very little pepper. Make sure it is nice and moist. Refrigerate for at least an hour and it's Yummy time!!   ❸

Italian Pasta Salad

1 box of rotini style whole wheat pasta
1 cup of brocolli slaw
1 cup of shredded carrots
1 cup of Italian Dressing (page 86)

Prepare the pasta according to the directions, al dente. Rinse with cold water. Add the remaining ingredients and stir well, refrigerate for an hour. YUMMY!! ❸

Toasted Pine Nut Pasta Salad

1 box of whole grain rotini pasta
1 bag of broccoli slaw
I small jar of sun dried tomatoes packed in olive oil
1 cup of shredded carrots
1 cup of pine nuts
2 cloves of garlic, crushed
¼ cup extra virgin olive oil
1 cup parmesan cheese (freshly grated)
½ cup fresh basil cut into strips
Sea salt
Pepper

Put coconut oil in a small skillet and heat. Once hot, add the pine nuts. Let them sit and then, after a few minutes, stir. Repeat for a few minutes until they have become lightly toasted. Cook your swirled pasta according to package directions, al dente. Rinse in cold water until the pasta becomes cold. In a large bowl, add the cold pasta, the sundried tomatoes with the liquid, the olive oil, and stir. Slowly add the remaining ingredients until everything is used up. Add sea salt and pepper to taste. FRESH!!! ❸

Hot Pasta

1 box of angel hair whole grain pasta
1 pint of cherry tomatoes (cut in half)
10 basil leaves (cut into strips)
2 crushed cloves of garlic
Red pepper flakes – to desired taste
Sea salt – to taste
¼ cup olive oil
1 cup spinach

Prepare pasta according to package directions. Drain. Put in a large skillet with garlic, olive oil, and red pepper flakes. Stir, and then add tomatoes, basil leaves, spinach, and salt to taste. Let simmer until the flavors have blended, about 15 minutes. Taste, test… Maybe add more red pepper flakes if you want a kick!! ❸

Family Favorite
Pasta Alfredo

1 14-oz. box of whole grain penne pasta
2 cloves of garlic crushed
¼ cup organic butter
3 Tbsp whole grain flour
¼ cup fresh basil
½ tsp sea salt (or more to taste)
½ tea pepper (or more to taste)
1-1 ½ cup organic milk
8 oz. Neufchatel cheese
1 ½ cup freshly grated parmesan cheese
½ tsp fresh parsley

Prepare the whole grain pasta according to package instructions. In a saucepan, combine the butter and garlic, sauté the garlic until browned. Add the flour and mix with a fork ensuring it becomes well blended. Add salt and pepper continuing to stir. Add ½ of the milk and stir until thickened, then add the rest. Watch the consistency and turn down the heat. Add ¼ of the Neufchatel cheese, stir until melted, continue until all of the cheese has been added. Mix in ½ of the parmesan cheese. Stir until melted and everything is blended well. Add the basil and mix. Combine the penne pasta with the cheese mixture. When you serve add the remaining parmesan cheese on top and the fresh parsley. Yummy!!! Serve with grilled asparagus! ❸

Herbs

Herbs, both fresh and dried, enhance the flavor of dishes! In general, you should add fresh herbs toward the end of cooking as their flavor dissipates with long exposure to heat; dried herbs may be used in dishes that cook longer, and measure for measure are much more concentrated in flavor than the fresh varieties.

Storing – Keep fresh herbs in water, as you would cut flowers. They will last for up to 1 week if trimmed daily and refrigerated. Store dried herbs in tightly covered containers in a cool dark place for up to 6 months.

Beef

In the past several years, we have learned that we should not eat animals that are injected with hormones, steroids, and antibiotics. If you have children, you should take into consideration the growth hormones and steroids that are given to animals that make up our food supply. Children are maturing at a faster rate than they did years ago. Children are also more obese today according to research. Studies continue to be done to prove that growth hormones and steroids that are in commercial meat and dairy products are impacting the health of our youth. If you have children, you should consider only feeding them hormone free beef and dairy products. This will allow their bodies to grow and develop naturally. Many people have decided to go without meat just for these reasons alone.

Beef Tenderloin Steak with Onions

1 large onion halved and sliced
2 tablespoons butter
⅓ cup white wine or chicken broth
1 garlic clove- minced
½ teaspoon dried rosemary, crushed
¼ teaspoon salt
¼ teaspoon pepper
2 beef tenderloin steaks, 1-1/2 to 2 inches thick

In a large skillet, cook onion in butter over medium heat for 15-20 minutes or until onion is golden brown, stirring frequently. Stir in wine or broth and garlic. Bring to a boil. Reduce heat; simmer uncovered, for 3-4 minutes or until liquid has evaporated. Meanwhile, combine the rosemary, salt, and pepper; rub over steaks. Broil 4 in. from the heat for 7-9 minutes on each side or until meat reaches desired doneness (for medium-rare, a meat thermometer should read 145°F; medium, 160°F; well-done, 170°F). Serve with caramelized onions.

Save one for later!—Freeze it!

Korean Beef

1 flank steak
Braggs Liquid Aminos
2 Tbsp toasted sesame oil
1 bunch green onions, finely chopped
6 cloves garlic, peeled and mashed
2 Tbsp sesame seeds
¼ tsp cayenne pepper

Using a very sharp and heavy knife, slice the flank steak as thinly as possible across the grain and on the diagonal. (This will be easier if the meat is partially frozen.) Mix other ingredients and marinate beef in the mixture, refrigerated, for several hours or overnight. Place on an electric griddle or broil until done. Can even be barbecued. Prepare with carrots and summer squash. ❶

Notes

Some healthy eating tips...

Try to buy organic when possible

Use meats that are hormone free

Try to prepare your own sauces staying clear of
extra additives and preservatives

Always read the ingredients

Raw or natural is best

Chicken & Turkey

Just like with the beef, there are reasons why you would want to purchase free range, organic chicken. To sell chicken labeled "organic," growers must comply with extremely high standards and get certified. The certification standards are becoming very hard and expensive to reach for local farmers and sadly many local farmers are going out of business. A great idea is to visit your local farms and ask the farmers for a tour of their facilities to see if their farm is a place that you would want to purchase your poultry from.

It could be confusing at the store level. You will see a lot of poultry that implies it is healthy. These labels include "natural" and "antibiotic-free." These terms are not regulated by a set of standards, nor do they require third-party inspection. Farms that raise these birds may or may not prioritize healthy standards that you are looking for.

Seasoned Grilled Chicken

Grill until cooked, or when the temperature of the chicken reaches 165°F. Prepare raw cabbage with oil and vinegar. You can use prepared Coleslaw mixes and mix it up with Balsamic Vinaigrette. ❶

Grilled Chicken with Veggies

Look in the prepared salad mixes section of your produce section at the store and grab a bag of mixed fresh vegetables. It contains broccoli, carrots, snow-peas, broccoli straw, and possibly cauliflower. Grill your chicken in a very small amount of smart balance oil in your electric frying pan, season first with sea salt and pepper. Add the package of fresh veggies. Sauté according to package directions. Add cold pressed sesame oil to add an Asian flavor. Sprinkle with sesame seeds on top. Prepare brown rice as a side. Chop red cabbage and toss with grated carrots, olive oil, and balsamic vinegar. ❶

Grilled Chicken with Salsa

1½ lb chicken breast, skinless
2 Tbsp coconut oil
Sea salt
Pepper
1 cup salsa
2 Tbsp cilantro
1 Tbsp chili powder
¼ cup water

In an electric skillet heat the coconut oil. Add the chicken breast when the pan has reached 350°F. Add sea salt, pepper, cilantro, and chili powder to both sides of the chicken. Grill for about 4-6 minutes per side or until the internal temperature of the chicken reaches 165°F. Add water to the pan and turn to low and simmer for a minute with the top on. Add salsa on the top of the chicken. In a separate double broiler, steam your favorite veggies as a side for this meal. ❶

Italian Baked Chicken

1½ lb chicken breast, skinless
Sea salt
Pepper
Italian Dressing

Pre-heat the oven to 400°F. In a glass 9x13 pan, place the chicken seasoned with sea salt and pepper. Add Italian Dressing as a marinade over chicken breast. Bake until the internal temperature of the chicken reaches 165°F. ❶

Oven Baked (not fried) Chicken

1½ chicken breast, skinless
3 Tbsp organic butter
1 tsp lemon pepper
1 tsp dill
1 tsp sage
2 Tbsp basil – slivered
Sea salt to taste
3-4 Tbsp whole grain flour

Take a 9 x 13 glass pan and put slivers of butter in the bottom of the pan. Lay your breast on top of the butter and add a little bit more on top of each breast. Season your chicken with sea salt, lemon pepper, dill, sage, slivers of basil, and add a little of whole grain flour on each breast. Bake your chicken at 400°F, checking periodically to make sure the top stays moist. When the internal temp reaches 165°F (approx, 40-45 min) it is ready...yum! Prepare a broccoli slaw with Balsamic Vinaigrette and some almond slivers. ❶

Baked Chicken and Sweet Potatoes

1½ chicken breast, skinless
2 Tbsp organic butter
Sea salt to taste
Pepper
Lemon juice from one lemon

Pre-heat the oven to 400°F. Season the skinless chicken breast with sea salt, pepper, lemon juice, and butter. Bake chicken on 400°F in a glass pan in oven. When the internal temp reaches 165°F (approx, 40-45 min) it is ready. ❷

Sweet Potatoes

3-4 sweet potatoes
2 Tbsp organic butter
2 Tbsp raw honey
2 tsp cinnamon

Clean 3-4 large sweet potatoes and pat dry. Lightly oil a glass baking dish. Peel and slice the potatoes (the short way, like potato chips but thicker) and lay them in a glass baking pan. Add a few slices of butter on the sweet potatoes and sprinkle cinnamon. Cook until the potatoes are tender, about 30 minutes. ❸

Chicken Kabobs with Veggies

½ boneless skinless chicken breast
1 pint of cherry tomatoes
1 pint of mushrooms
1 red bell pepper
1 green bell pepper
2 cloves of minced garlic
1 small onion.
½ cup lemon juice
½ cup olive oil
1 tsp salt
1 tsp pepper
¼ cup water

Cut chicken into small cubes and marinate in a mixture of lemon juice, garlic, water, salt, and pepper for 30 minutes. When ready, place the chicken and veggies on skewers as you prefer. Grill or broil until chicken is cooked through. Serve with a healthy side of your choice. Of course that would include a small dinner salad, too. ❷

Fire Roasted Chicken with Tomatoes

1½ boneless skinless chicken breast
2 Tbsp coconut oil
Sea salt
Pepper
1 tsp basil
1 tsp oregano
2 Tbsp lemon balm
2 15-oz. cans of fire roasted tomatoes

In an electric skillet heat the coconut oil. Add the chicken breast when the pan has reached 350°F. Add sea salt and pepper to each side of the skinless chicken breast. Grill the chicken for a few minutes on each side and then add the basil, oregano, and lemon balm to the chicken. After a few more minutes, add both cans of fire roasted tomatoes. Turn down to low and simmer until finished. This is a great paired up with Basmati Rice. ❷

Cilantro Lime Chicken Cacciatore
2 lb. chicken breast sliced into 1 oz. cubes
1 Tbsp minced garlic
½ cup fresh squeezed lime juice
3 Tbsp chopped cilantro
2 Tbsp extra virgin olive oil
5 medium roma tomatoes
Sea salt to taste
Cayenne pepper to taste

Heat sauté pan to medium. Add olive oil, garlic, cilantro, and ¼ cup of lime juice, simmer for 4-6 minutes. While simmering, pour ¼ cup of lime juice over chicken; let stand for ½ a minute. Season chicken with sea salt and pepper. After 4-6 minutes, add seasoned chicken to the pan and cook for 8-10 minutes over medium heat, until done. ❶

Roasted Pastured Chicken
1 pastured chicken, whole, 4-5 pounds (a broiler)
1 apple, small
1 onion, small
1 stalk celery, plus leaves
1 sprig rosemary, 3"
¼ cup chicken broth
Celtic sea salt
Pepper, freshly ground

Rinse and drain your thawed chicken. Preheat the oven to 350°F. Quarter and core the apple. Peel and quarter onion. Slice celery into 2-3" pieces. Add the chicken broth to the cavity of the bird. Stuff the chicken with apple, celery, onion, and rosemary. Sprinkle bird with salt and freshly ground pepper and rub them into the skin. Place chicken in a baking dish with 2" sides. Bake approximately 1½ hours or until a meat thermometer reads 180°F when pushed into the thigh. During the cooking, spoon chicken broth from the bottom of the pan and pour onto the chicken. Do this a few times. Remove the chicken from the oven and allow to rest for approximately 20 minutes before carving. The rest period allows the juices to redistribute and results in more tender meat. ❶

Prepare veggies of your choice.

Pineapple Chicken

4 breasts of chicken
Sea salt
Pepper
1 tsp dried thyme
2 Tbsp coconut oil
8-oz. can of pinapple chunks in juice

In an electric skillet, heat up the coconut oil. Add the chicken and season with sea salt and pepper. Flip and season the other side. Let cook until it is done. Take out of the pan and slice the chicken on an angle. Use paper towels to wipe out the pan, make sure there is no oil, then place the Chicken back into the pan. Add the pineapple chunks with the juice. Heat it on low for about 15 minutes. Great served with Raw Veggies and Basmati Rice. ❸

Turkey Loaf

1 lb of lean ground turkey,
½ cup of steal cut oats
1 omega-3 egg
1 tsp onion powder
1 tsp paprika
2 tsp fresh-cut parsley
Sea salt
Pepper
1 tsp garlic powder
1 6-oz. can organic tomato paste

Beat the egg in a small bowl. In a large bowl combine the turkey with the remaining ingredients and mix well. Add the egg to the mixture. Once everything is mixed thoroughly, shape your meat mixture into a loaf. Cook it at 350 for 30-35 minutes or until internal temperature reaches 165°F. About 15 minutes before it is finished, open a can of organic tomato paste and spread it on top of your loaf with a butter knife (not the sides). Finish cooking.

Prepare lightly steamed asparagus and summer squash sprinkled with parsley for your side dish. ❷

Family Favorite
Chicken Enchilladas
2 lbs. of chicken
2 Tbsp coconut oil
2½ cups of Enchilada Sauce (page 88)
Bunch of fresh cilantro
Filtered water
Raw Monterey Jack cheese
Raw cheddar cheese
½ cup chopped scallions
Sea salt
Pepper

Pre-heat the oven to 400°F. Put the coconut oil in a heavy skillet, on medium heat. When warm, add the finely diced onions. When they are soft, add the chicken and season with salt and pepper. Cover with the lid half way off. After a few minutes, flip the chicken, season the other side, and add a hand full of fresh cilantro on top. Cover and let sit for about 3 minutes. Cook until completely done. Take the chicken out of the pot and put on a cutting board. With a sharp knife, shred the chicken. Put the chicken back into the heavy skillet with the onions and cover with enchilada sauce. Let simmer for about 15 minutes.

In another skillet, lightly oil the pan with coconut oil. Take each tortilla, one or two at a time and heat it, then flip it until you get through all the tortillas. Set out two 9 x 13 glass pans and pour ½ cup of enchilada sauce into each one. Next, take each tortilla and dip it in to the enchilada sauce then take the the chicken mixture and fill each tortilla, put a little cheese in each one (raw cheese is strong so only a little bit). Roll the tortilla and chicken mixture tightly and place in the glass pan. You should be able to fit 14 in each dish. Spread cheese and scallions on top of the pan. For my family, I just put scallions on ¼ of one pan, because some of the people here would prefer no scallions. (It works!) Then, add additional sauce to cover the top. SUPPER YUMMY. ❸

Italian Turkey Sausage

2 lbs of turkey sausage
1 onion
½ yellow bell pepper
½ red bell pepper
½ tsp of pepper
½ tsp of pepper
½ tsp salt
½ tsp garlic powder
½ tsp sage

Finely dice your peppers and onions. I have a small food processor that does the trick, or use a hand chopper. The finer, the better. Combine all of your ingredients together in a bowl and mix very well. Get your hands in it. Just like Mama used to make meat loaf. Mix it, mix it good! Cover the bowl and refrigerate for about ½-1 hour and let the seasonings blend into the turkey. ❶

For Spaghetti

Take the above mixture and brown your turkey sausage in a skillet. Add spaghetti sauce when finished. Boil whole grain spaghetti according to package directions. ❸

For Meatballs

2 eggs
1 cup steel cut oats

Take the turkey sausage meat mixture and add the eggs and the oats to it. Mix it well. Shape into 2-inch meatballs. Slightly oil a 9 x13 glass baking dish with a paper towel. Place the meatballs inside. Bake at 400°F for about 30 minutes or until the meatballs have reached an internal temperature of 165°F. ❷

Use the meatballs for a spaghetti dish or for a meatball crockpot dish.

Turkey Sausage

1 lb ground turkey
2 tsp garlic
1 ½ crushed fennel seed
1 tsp salt
1 tsp dried oregano
1 tsp dried sage

Mix it all together and shape into turkey patties. Refrigerate for 8 hours or overnight. ❶

Marinated Turkey

Small turkey breast
Sea salt
Pepper
Basil
Lemon juice from 1 lemon
Cider vinegar

Season your turkey breast with sea salt, pepper, and basil. Squeeze lemon juice over it very generously, along with a little cider vinegar. Refrigerate for at least 1 hour. Bake at 350 for 20-30 minutes until the internal temperature reaches 165°F. Prepare with steamed green peas, carrots and onions. ❷

My Favorite Herbs

Sage

Oregano

Thyme

Lemon Balm

Cinnamon

Mint

Fish

When it comes to fish, you should purchase wild caught fish. It is natural, antibiotic free, not ejected with artificial colors, less fatty, and has a higher level of omega-3 fatty acids (the good fats). Fish continues to be a great source of protein, and is very satisfying. It is recommended to eat fish three times a week, giving the other "meat guys" a break.

Orange Roughy

Orange roughy fillets
1 tsp dill
Sea salt
Pepper
1 lemon

Take frozen wild caught orange roughy and cook according to package directions. Prior to cooking, add dill, sea salt, and pepper to season. Halfway through the cooking time, add sliced lemons to the top of each piece of orange roughy and squeeze remaining lemon over each piece. Finish baking.

As the fish is baking, slice fresh Roma tomatoes, arrange on a plate and drizzle olive oil over top and sprinkle with oregano, dash of sea salt, and pepper to taste. ❶

Marinated Orange Roughy with Sweet Potatoes

Orange Roughy fillets
1 tsp. dill
Sea salt
Pepper
1 cup Balsamic Vinaigrette Dressing

Season fish with dill, sea salt, pepper, marinate the orange roughy in Balsamic Vinaigrette for 30 minutes in the refrigerator. Bake or Broil until done.

Serve with sweet potatoes baked with cinnamon and butter and sautéed spinach. ❷

Baked Halibut

Frozen wild cut halibut
1 tsp dill
Sea salt
Pepper
Lemon

Take frozen wild caught halibut and cook according to package directions. Prior to cooking, add dill, sea salt, and pepper to season. Halfway through the cooking time, add sliced lemons to the top of each piece of halibut and squeeze remaining lemon over each piece. Finish baking.

As the fish is baking, slice fresh roma tomatoes, arrange on a plate and drizzle olive oil over top and sprinkle with oregano, dash of sea-salt, and pepper to taste. ❶

Grilled Salmon

Use wild caught salmon and prepare just as the halibut above. ❶

Teriyaki Salmon

2 Tbsp lemon juice
2 Tbsp Braggs Amino Liquid
¼ tsp ground mustard
¼ tsp ground ginger
⅛ tsp garlic powder
2 (6-oz.) Salmon fillets

In a shallow glass container, combine the first five ingredients; mix well. Set aside ½ cup for basting and refrigerate. Add salmon to remaining marinade; cover and refrigerate for 30 min. If you can do longer—great! Drain and discard the marinade. Place the salmon on a broiler pan. Broil 3-4 inches from the heat for 5 minutes. Brush with reserved marinade; turn and broil for 5 minutes or until fish flakes easily with a fork. Brush with marinade. ❶

Sesame Salmon

2 tsp Braggs Amino liquid
2 tsp sesame oil
Sea salt
Pepper
1 garlic cloves, minced
Sesame seeds

Mix cold pressed sesame oil and Braggs Amino Liquid in a bowl and set aside. Season the salmon with sea salt, pepper, minced garlic and sesame seeds. Place the salmon on a broiler pan. Broil 3-4 inches from the heat for 5 minutes. Turn the oven off when the salmon is finished and place the mixture of sesame oil and Braggs Amino Liquid over the salmon. Put in the oven for about 1 minute, just enough time to get the liquid warm.

Stir-fry an Asian mix of veggies! Use snow peas, broccoli, carrots, red peppers, and a few green and yellow peppers as well, mushrooms and bamboo shoots. You can find this mixture pre-packaged if you would like. ❶

Grilled Salmon

3 oz. salmon
Juice of 1 lemon
1 Tbsp of butter
Sea salt
Pepper
1clove of garlic, crushed
1 tsp oregano

Add the juice of an entire lemon and a tablespoon of butter to an electric grill. Place 3 oz. of salmon in the grill on the top of the butter and lemon mixture. Season your salmon with sea salt, pepper, fresh garlic, and oregano. Grill until done. Add some fresh spinach to the pan and sauté with lemon juice and extra virgin olive oil, a little bit of garlic would be great too! ❶

Oven Roasted Salmon

1 salmon filet (2 – 2½ lbs), skin on
3 cloves garlic, minced
2 tsp finely chopped fresh thyme
Sea salt
Freshly ground black pepper
2 Tbsp fresh lemon juice
2 Tbsp extra-virgin olive oil
Dab of organic raw butter

Position a rack in the upper ⅔ of the oven and preheat to 450°F. Use a glass baking dish and coat the dish with lemon juice, rubbed with a little butter as well. Place the salmon, skin side down, in the pan. Rub the garlic all over the flesh side of the salmon, sprinkle the rosemary and thyme, and then season with sea salt and pepper. Drizzle with the lemon juice. Roast the salmon for 14- 20 minutes, depending on the thickness of the fish. The salmon is done when the thickest part of the fillet flakes easily when tested with a fork, or an instant read thermometer registers 140°F when inserted into the thickest part of the fillet. Take out of the oven and drizzle with the olive oil. ❶

Serve on a long platter and surround with Yummy steamed vegetables.

Tilapia

Fresh or frozen wild caught tilapia
1 tsp dill
Sea salt
Pepper
Juice of 1 lemon
½ Tbsp of raw butter

Squeeze ½ of the juice of a lemon in a 13x9 glass shallow baking dish and add a little butter. Place the tilapia in the baking dish and season it with sea salt, pepper and dill. Bake in the oven at 350°F until flaky and tender and the internal temperature reaches 145°F. ❶

Tuna Steak

1½ lb tuna steaks
2 Tbsp coconut oil
2 tsp finely chopped ginger root
2 tsp sea salt
⅛ tsp ground red cayenne pepper
2 cloves of crushed garlic
freshly squeezed lime juice of 1 lime

Marinate 1½ lb of tuna steaks in: ¼ cup lime juice, 2 Tbsp olive oil, 2 tsp finely chopped ginger root, 2 tsp sea salt, ⅛ tsp ground red cayenne pepper, 2 cloves of crushed garlic, and freshly squeezed juice of 1 lime. Leave in the fridge for at least 1 hour. The fish may stay for up to 24 hours in the fridge. Cover and grill, add additional marinade, turning once. Cook until fish flakes easily with a fork. Discard remaining marinade. Serve with lime wedges and sautéed spinach with fresh garlic and almonds. ❶

Notes

Crock Pot Recipes

A lot can be done in the crock pot and this is an area where you can become very creative. Have you ever just thrown 8-10 small potatoes in the crock pot with a little garlic, sea salt and pepper, turned it on low and then went on with your day? Arriving home to eating nice garlic baked potatoes, with a little crunch on the bottom. Crock pots are very convenient for the busy family. You can come home to a completely cooked meal.

Southwestern Chicken

1 cup lime juice
5 cups chicken, boneless, skinless breast (cut-up)
1 jar 24-oz. salsa
1 or 2 cans chopped green chilies, not drained
3 Tbsp chili powder
⅛ tsp cumin
Pinch of oregano
1- 2 cloves minced garlic
1 small finely diced onion
Cilantro, finely chopped
1 24-oz. can black beans drained (1½ cups of beans)
1 24-oz. can red kidney beans drained (1½ cups of beans)
2 cups summer squash or zucchini, in small cubes
⅓ cup raw organic cheddar cheese or plain Greek yogurt. (for garnish)

Partially thaw the chicken and chop into bite sized pieces.

Marinate the chicken all night in lime juice for extra tenderness and a zesty flavor.

Place chicken in crockpot

Then pour in remaining ingredients over the chicken. (Except squash and garnish)

Simmer on high for 4 hours or on low for 6 hours.

20-30 minutes before serving add the squash or zucchini.

Garnish with raw grated cheese, Greek yogurt, and optional cilantro. ❶

Barbequed Meatballs

Use the meatballs recipe on page 58.

Take cooked meatballs and put them in a crockpot on low with a good amount of barbeque sauce to completely cover the top. Cook on low for about 1 hour. ❷

Lemon Herbed Roasted Chicken

4-5 lb whole chicken
1 lemon, juiced
½ tsp sea salt
½ tsp pepper
½ small onion finely diced
1 Tbsp fresh parsley
1 Tbsp fresh sage
¼ tsp thyme
¼ tsp paprika

Rinse chicken and pat dry well. Season the chicken with all of the seasonings and then put into the crock pot. Squeeze the lemon over the entire chicken and then top with onions. Turn the crock pot on low for 8-10 hours, or high for 4-5 hours. The chicken will create a wonderful broth. ❶

Taco-Roni

1 lb of ground turkey
1 small onion, chopped
¾ cup water
2 Tbsp dried cilantro
¼ cup chili powder
1 15-oz. can tomato sauce
1 package (8 oz.) whole wheat macaroni, uncooked
1 4-oz. can mild chopped green chili & tomato mixture
1½ - 2 cups mild shredded raw cheddar cheese

In a heavy pan brown the ground turkey and add the onion. Transfer it to the crockpot and add the remaining ingredients with the exception of the cheese. Cook on low for 6-8 hours and or high 3-4 hours. In the last 30 minutes top Taco-Roni with shredded cheese. ❸

Soups

Soups are not just for the winter months. They are great way to get a full satisfying meal in one bowl. Soups can be made ahead of time, frozen, and taken out to eat when you may not be prepared to cook. They are always satisfying and filling.

Yummy Veggie Soup

(Many clients favorite)

14-16 oz. bag of frozen organic vegetables
2 14-oz. can organic tomatoes with garlic
2 14-oz. cans of vegetable broth
1 clove of garlic crushed
1 tsp of oregano

Put everything in the crock pot and let it cook on low all day. ❶

Lentil Sausage Soup

½ lb dry lentils
2 Tbsp butter
½ onion – diced
1 cups carrots – diced
2 leeks, white part only, diced
½ cup celery – diced
½ lb Italian turkey sausage
1 quarts chicken broth
2 Tbsp Dijon mustard (or 4 if you like it flavorful)
1 Tbsp red wine vinegar (or more if you like it flavorful)
½ cup organic milk
Little salt and pepper to taste
1 cups spinach (fresh spinach shredded into thin strips)

Rinse lentils and soak for 2-5 hours in plenty of cool water. Drain and rinse again after soaking.

Melt butter and sauté onions, carrots, leeks, and celery until softened. Add to pot with chicken broth and lentils. Brown sausage breaking into pieces – drain on paper towel and add to broth. Bring to a boil. Reduce heat to simmer and cook for approximately 45-55 minutes. (Be sure lentils are cooked.)

Add mustard, red wine vinegar, milk, salt, and pepper. Cook an additional 10 minutes – adjust seasonings to taste. Add spinach, simmer 30 seconds and serve. (Can be made a day ahead.) ❷

Organic Tomato Basil Bisque

3 14.5-oz. cans of organic diced tomatoes
1 medium onion
8 cloves of fresh garlic (chopped)
1 Tbsp olive oil
¼ cup water
1 cup organic milk (or heavy cream)
2 Tbsp of basil (fresh chopped or dried)
Pinch of salt and pepper to taste

Heat 1 Tbsp of olive oil in a pan over medium heat and grill onions until golden brown. Add chopped garlic when onions are half way done and grill until golden. When onions and garlic are golden, add ¼ cup water and continue to cook for 5 minutes. Remove from heat. Open cans of diced tomatoes and put into food processor or blender and blend until smooth. Pour tomatoes into a 3-qt soup pot and add onions with garlic. Over medium heat, bring to a boil. Add basil, salt and pepper, and continue to boil for 5 minutes. Add 1 cup organic milk at the end, stir and serve! This delicious bisque takes less than 20 minutes to prepare and tastes delicious! ❸

Black Bean Taco Soup

1 lb organic ground beef
1 onion, chopped
1 14-16 oz bag of frozen organic corn,
2 14-16oz. cans black beans
1 16-oz can of tomato sauce
2 cans (14-16 oz.) or 1 can 28 oz. fire roasted tomatoes
1 Tbsp chili powder
½ Tbsp onion powder
2 cups water
Use Salsa, 1 sliced avocado or plain Greek yogurt as a topping.

Sauté beef and onion until browned and cooked through. Add all remaining ingredients with the seasonings and water and heat thoroughly. Turn to low and let simmer for 20 minutes. This is easy, high in fiber and healthy. ❸

Cauliflower Vegetable Soup with Feta

2 Tbsp extra virgin coconut oil
1 cup chopped yellow onion
1½ tsp minced garlic
6 cups cauliflower florets (6 cups = about 1 large head)
½ cup chopped carrot
½ cup chopped celery
1 Tbsp finely chopped Serrano chili pepper
2 cans (14-oz. each) organic chicken broth
1 can (14.5-oz. each) organic diced tomatoes with sweet onions, undrained
1 bay leaf
½ tsp ground cumin
¼ tsp sea salt
¼ tsp coarse ground black pepper
6 Tbsp crumbled feta cheese

Heat oil in large saucepan over medium-high heat until hot. Add onions and garlic. Cook 2 to 3 minutes or until onions are translucent, stirring often. Add cauliflower, carrots, celery, and chili pepper; cook 4 minutes or until cauliflower begins to brown, stirring often. Add broth, undrained tomatoes, bay leaf, cumin, salt, and black pepper. Bring to a boil. Cover and reduce heat to medium-low; cook 15 to 20 minutes or until cauliflower is tender, stirring occasionally. Remove and discard bay leaf before serving.

Sprinkle 1 tablespoon feta cheese on top of each serving. ❷

Cold Cucumber-Avocado Soup

1 cucumber, seeded and chopped
2 ripe avocados, sliced
½ cup fresh cilantro
2 Tbsp green onion, chopped
2 small serrano peppers (optional)
½ cup Greek yogurt
2 cup veggie stock
¼ cup lime juice
Salt and pepper to taste
Cayenne pepper to taste

Put everything except cayenne in the blender and blend until combined, with a little texture (or you can blend until totally smooth, if you like). Add the cayenne into individual bowl, to individual's taste. Garnish with a little cilantro and small dollop of Greek yogurt. ❷

Broccoli and Cheese Soup

16 oz. frozen broccoli pieces
12 oz. frozen cauliflower pieces
2 cup water
2 cup chicken broth
1 cup chopped celery
1 cup chopped carrots
1 tsp salt
½ tsp pepper
3 Tbsp whole grain flour
2 cups organinc skim milk
8 oz. shredded raw cheddar cheese

In a large pot, combine, water, vegetables, broth, salt, and pepper. Bring to a boil and simmer until the vegetables are tender (15-20 min.) In a separate bowl, blend flour and milk. Slowly add flour/milk mixture to the large pot. Stir constantly until soup thickens. Add cheese and stir until melted and smooth. ❷

Potato and Broccoli Soup

8 small red potatoes
1 cup raw cheddar cheese
5 cup crispy steamed broccoli (lightly cooked)
2 15-oz cans of organic vegetable broth
1 cup organic milk
½ small diced onion
2 Tbsp parsley
A pinch sea salt
Pepper to taste
4 slices cooked turkey bacon, crumbled

Dice and boil the potatoes. When the potatoes are almost done, add the broccoli and the onion. Lightly cook the broccoli so it remains crisp. Drain and set aside 1 cup of the potato broth. In a separate sauce pan, heat up on medium heat the vegetable broth, milk, sea salt, parsley and cheese until you have a nice cheese mixture. Add the cheese mixture to the potato mixture, using as much of the potato broth as needed. Simmer on low for 15 minutes and add the turkey bacon right before serving. ❸

Herbed Split Pea Soup

16 oz. dried green or yellow split peas
5 oz. slivered turkey ham – no nitrates
5 tsp olive oil
1⅓ cup carrots, sliced
2½ tsp dried marjoram
¼ tsp black pepper
1⅓ cup chopped onion
3 garlic cloves minced
1 tsp salt

Sort and rinse peas. Place in a 3-quart pan; cover with 2" water and bring to a boil. Remove from heat; cover. Let stand 1 hour; drain. In the same pan, heat oil, add onions, carrots, and garlic. Sauté until soft, about 5 minutes. Add peas and 4 cups water. Bring to a boil; reduce heat. Simmer covered, 1 hour or until peas are tender, stirring once. Add turkey ham, marjoram, salt, and pepper and heat to serving temperature. Soup thickens upon standing. When reheating, add additional water to thin. ❷

Chickpea and Sweet-Potato Stew

2 tsp extra-virgin olive oil
½ cup chopped onion
½ cup chopped celery
3 cups water
1 (15 oz.) can chickpeas, rinsed and drained
1 medium sweet potato, peeled and diced
1 (14.5 oz.) can fire-roasted diced tomatoes
1 bay leaf
½ tsp tumeric
½ tsp ground cinnamon
½ tsp ground cumin
Salt and pepper to taste

Heat the oil over medium heat in a 3-quart pot with a lid. Add the onion and celery, stir and cook until the onion is translucent, about 2 minutes. Add the water and all remaining ingredients.

Cover the pot, raise heat to high, and bring the stew to a boil. Uncover the pot, reduce heat to medium, and cook at a slow boil until the sweet potatoes are tender, about 20 minutes. Serve immediately or simmer until ready to serve. ❷

Tomato Bacon Soup

1 pound turkey bacon, chopped
1 small onion, chopped
3 cloves garlic, peeled, finely chopped
2 cans (14.5-oz each) diced tomatoes fire roasted tomatoes, undrained
1 can (14-oz each) organic chicken broth
1 can (6-oz each) organic tomato paste
1 cup heavy organic (whipping) cream
½ cup coarsely chopped fresh basil, divided
1 clove of diced garlic
½ cup of chopped oregano

Heat a little coconut oil in a large saucepan over medium-high heat until hot. Add bacon; cook 5 to 10 minutes or until crisp. Remove bacon. Reduce heat to medium; add onion and cook 5 minutes or until translucent. Add garlic; cook 1 minute more or until fragrant.

Stir in undrained tomatoes, broth, and tomato paste. Bring to a boil, reduce heat to low and simmer 20 minutes, stirring occasionally.

Stir in cream; simmer 10 minutes, stirring frequently. Add half of the basil to the tomato mixture. Remove soup from heat. Place a portion in blender container. Puree 1 to 2 minutes or until smooth. Repeat until all soup is pureed.

Place bisque in serving bowls; top with the remaining bacon and basil.

This bisque can be made a day ahead. Prepare entirely except for heavy cream. The next day, heat bisque over medium heat until warm and stir in cream. ❸

Red Meat Chili

1½ lb ground beef
1 onion, finely chopped
2 small green chilies, hot or mild, seeded and chopped
2 cans 14.5-15 oz. tomatoes, briefly chopped in food processer
1 clove garlic, peeled and mashed
½ Tbsp ground cumin
½ Tbsp dried oregano
1 Tbsp dried basil
¼ to ½ tsp red chili flakes
3 14.5-15 oz. cans kidney beans
Organic blue chips for garnish
Chopped green onions for garnish
Greek yogurt for garnish
Avocado slices for garnish
Chopped cilantro for garnish

Brown meat until it is crumbly at medium heat in a heavy pot. Drain, and add remaining ingredients. Simmer about 1 hour. Serve with garnishes. ❷

White Bean Turkey Stew

1 can (14.5 oz.) organic chicken broth
2 cups organic shredded carrots
2 cans (15.5 oz. each) white beans, drained and rinsed
3 cups cubed cooked turkey
¼ cup chopped parsley
½ cup red and green peppers, thinly sliced
¼ cup onion
¼ cup grated parmesan cheese

In a lightly oiled pan, (coconut oil) sauté peppers and onion until onions are translucent. Add ½ of your parsley and organic broth and bring chicken broth mixture to a simmer in a large saucepan. Add carrots and one can of the beans; mash second can of beans and add to saucepan.

Stir in turkey. Cover and simmer 5 minutes. Stir in parmesan and remaining parsley. ❶

White Bean Chicken Chili

2 lbs chicken skinless, boneless, breast
Coconut oil
2 cloves of finely chopped garlic
½ tsp of cumin
1 large onion coarsely chopped
Pepper
Sea salt
3 Tbsp dried cilantro
3 Tbsp of chili powder
6-oz. can of organic tomato sauce
2 15-oz. cans of fire roasted tomatoes (undrained)
2 15-oz. cans of water (use the tomato cans)
½ cup water
2 14.5- or 15.0-oz cans of great northern beans (drained and rinsed)
Organic sour cream (use as a garnish)
Cilantro (use as a garnish)

Lightly oil your heavy skillet with organic coconut oil. Heat it up on medium and add the cloves and onions. Cook until onions are translucent and clear. While the onions and garlic are cooking, season your chicken lightly with pepper, sea salt, cumin, and cilantro. After the onions and garlic are coming to a finish, add the chicken breast, and cook evenly on both sides until nicely browned and internal temperatures reach 165°F. When the chicken is done, dice it and then add it back to the pan with the tomatoes. Turn the heavy pan to low, or simmer and add ½ cup of water. Boy your kitchen smells good, doesn't it? While the chicken and extras are doing their thing, pull out a large pot and add the 2 cans of water (using your tomato cans), tomato paste, chili powder, beans, and the chicken mixture. Bring all to a boil, and then simmer for 30 minutes. Top each serving with organic sour cream; sprinkle with additional fresh cilantro. ❷

Information on Nuts

Many varieties of nuts may be used to add rich flavor, protein, and crunchy texture to many dishes. Purchase nuts in small quantities that you'll use in a few months. Store in a dry, covered container.

Almonds – High in omega-3 fats with a mellow sweet flavor.

Pine Nuts – These are very good toasted on pastas and salads. A small ivory seed extracted from the cones of a species of pine tree with a rich flavor.

Walnuts – Are a rich crisp-textured nut which are good raw or toasted and also a good source of omega-3 fats.

To Toast Nuts

Toasting brings out the full flavor and aroma of nuts. To toast any kind of shelled nut, preheat an oven to 325°F. Spread the nuts in a single layer on a baking sheet and toast in the oven, stirring once, until they just begin to change color, 5-10 minutes. Alternatively toast nuts in a dry heavy frying pan over low heat, shaking and stirring to prevent scorching.

Snacks

A lot of people may tell you to watch your snacking if you want to lose weight. I will tell you a little different. Snack! Eat 6 small meals a day, which includes 3 snacks. Have a mid-morning snack, mid-afternoon snack, and an after dinner snack. Most of my clients get hungry during the mid-afternoon time. This makes them super hungry for dinner and they overeat. Snacking allows you to break up the larger meals and to spread it out along the day. Snacking will help to keep your body full of energy throughout the day. This way, you won't have highs and lows. Your blood sugar will stay more consistent. Snacks should be healthy. Trail mix, fruit, or veggies, but refuse the candy bar.

Trail Mix

1 cup raw pecans
1 cup raw cashews
1 cup unsulphured dried apricots, apples, pears, or pineapple cut into pieces
1 cup raisins
1 cup dried sweet coconut meat

Mix all together and store in an air tight container.

Makes 5-6 cups

Peanut Butter Nutty Bars

½ cup of raw honey
2 Tbsp coconut butter
1 ½ cup peanut butter
3 cups of oatmeal
¼ cup of wheat germ
¾ cups of raisins
½ cup of slivered almonds
½ cup of raw sunflower seeds

Preheat the oven to 350°F. Heat the honey, coconut butter, and peanut butter in a saucepan until ingredients are mixed well and melted together. Stir and then remove from heat. Add the oatmeal and wheat germ and mix well. Then add the raisins and almonds and seeds. Mix well. Press into a 9 inch square pan. Place into the oven and bake for 15 minutes until they are golden on the top. Allow to cool, cut into 12 squares and here is the perfect healthy snack.

***My kids prefer it without the fruit, so I add more sunflower seeds and almonds to make up for the raisins. My husband and I love it with the raisins! ❷

Fruit Wedges

Apple slices
Almond Butter

Core and cut your apple with an apple slicer in to 8 equal parts. Spread almond butter on top! ❷

Pumpkin Almond Bars

½ cup of raw honey
2 Tbsp coconut butter
1 ½ cup almond butter
½ cup can of pumpkin
¼ cup unsweetened apple sauce
3 ½ cups of oatmeal
¼ cup of wheat germ
¾ cups of raisins
½-¾ cup of slivered almonds
½-¾ cup of raw sunflower seeds

Heat the raw honey, coconut butter, almond butter, pumpkin, and apple sauce until all is blended well together. Mix with remaining ingredients and place into a 9-inch square pan. Place into the oven and bake for 25-30 minutes. Watch it closely to check for doneness. Allow to cool, cut into 12 squares and enjoy. ❷

Yummy Balls

(No- Bake)

½ cup raw honey
2 Tbsp coconut butter
1½ cashew butter
3 cups oatmeal
2 scoops of vanilla protein powder
1 tea cinnamon
½ cup coarsely chopped dried apple or raisins
½ cup slivered almonds
½ cup sunflower seeds

Heat the raw honey, coconut butter, and cashew butter in a saucepan until ingredients are mixed well together. Remove from heat. Add the remaining ingredients, and mix well. With a large spoon, scoop out the mixture into 2-inch balls. Place the Yummy balls on a cookie sheet; make sure the sides do not touch. Refrigerate for about 1 hour and then enjoy these energy snacks! ❷

Snack Ideas

Veggie Sticks ❶
  Carrots
  Celery
  Broccoli Florets

Sugar

Most people either have a sugar craving or a salt craving. For those that are addicted to sugar, I would recommend looking into a sugar detox. Meals, snacks, dressings, and sauces are loaded down with sugar today. Let me give you a few sugar facts:

Sugars contribute to obesity, sugars can cause varicose veins, sugar can cause hyperactivity, anxiety, difficulty in concentrating, and crankiness in children. Cancerous cells feed off of sugar. And research has shown that sugar can lead to diabetes.

For information on helping with sugar detoxification visit: www.myhealthkick.com

Dressings, Sauces & Marinades

Homemade dressings, sauces, and marinades are the key to controlling extra sugary condiments. You can still enjoy mayonnaise when you know the ingredients. When you make them yourself, you know there aren't any additives you would rather do without. As with anything, keep your portions in line and don't go over-board. Dressings, sauces, and marinades really make the meal taste great.

Balsamic Dressing

1 tsp Dijon-type dressing, smooth or grainy
2 Tbsp plus 1 tsp balsamic vinegar
½ cup extra virgin olive oil
½ tsp sage

Whisk all of the ingredients together and you've got yourself a winning dressing! ❶

Sesame Dressing

¼ cup sesame oil
½ cup olive oil
1 tsp Dijon mustard
2 Tbsp rice vinegar
2 pinches of sesame seeds

Mix it all in a shaker bottle, until well blended. ❶

Italian Dressing

1 ½ cup extra virgin olive oil
¾ - 1 cup rice vinegar
2 Tbsp water
1 cushed garlic clove
⅛ cup minced red onion
½ Tbsp raw honey
1 Tbsp dried oregano
½ tsp pepper
½ tsp dried thyme
½ tsp dried basil
½ tsp dried parsley
½ Tbsp sea salt

Mix it all in a shaker bottle, until well blended. Taste….Yummy! ❶

Ranch Dressing

1 cup mayonnaise (your homemade)
½ cup sour cream (organic)
½ cup buttermilk (organic)
2 cloves of finely chopped garlic
¼ finely chopped parsley
2 Tbsp finely chopped fresh chives
Sea salt to taste
Pepper to taste

Whisk all of the above ingredients together. Use your buttermilk to soften the flavors if necessary. Taste the dressing with a carrot stick. If it's good..move on.. if you're missing something…keep playing. Pour into a bottle for easy serving. Store in the refrigerator in a cold section. ❷

Mayonnaise

1½ cup olive oil
1 tsp sea salt
2 tsp (or to taste) lemon juice
1 organic cage free egg + 1 yolk
1 tsp mustard

In a blender or a food processor, add the egg + the extra yolk, the mustard, and the salt. Slowly add the oil, in a steady stream, until finished. Then add the lemon juice. This should take about 10 minutes to make as the mayo needs to thicken, and you don't want it to break. Store the Mayo in the fridge for 30 days in the coldest part. It is recommended to put it on a bottom shelf in the back. The door is too warm. YOU mean I can have Mayo??? If you make it yourself. ❷

Salsa

4 medium tomatoes, peeled, seeded , and diced
2 small onions, finely diced
⅛ cup chili powder
1 bunch cilantro, chopped
1 tsp dried oregano
Juice of 2 lemons
2 Tbsp sea salt
½ cup filtered water

Mix all of the ingredients and enjoy. ❶

Buffalo Sauce

¼ cup of ground cayenne pepper
1 tsp garlic powder
1 tsp onion powder
¼-½ tsp sea salt
⅛ cup rice vinegar
¼ cup filtered water

Put all of the above ingredients in a shaker bottle and shake, shake, shake away! Taste, and adjust accordingly. ❶

Enchilada Sauce

1 6-oz. can of organic tomato paste
¼ cup of chili powder
1 Tbsp of garlic powder
2 Tbsp of onion powder
2 cups filtered water

Heat all ingredients on medium heat until blended, then take it to a boil, then return to simmer. Taste it and adjust accordingly. ❶

Chipotle Sauce

1 cup Greek yogurt
1 cup mayonnaise (page 89)
½ tsp sea salt
¼ lime, zest and juice
1 chipotle chile, pureed
¼ cup guajillo chilies, chopped

Take all of the ingredients and mix in a blender until smooth. This is great with fish, southwestern wraps, or on salad to give a zesty taste. ❷

Spicy Orange Marinade

Great with chicken.

½ cup freshly squeezed orange juice
½ tsp Dijon mustard
2 Tbsp cider vinegar
2 Tbsp raw honey
2 Tbsp olive oil
1 clove garlic, finely chopped

Combine all ingredients in a small saucepan and simmer 3 minutes over low heat. Use immediately or store in an airtight container in the refrigerator for up to a week. Makes about 1/4 cup. ❶

Beefy Pepper Marinade

2 Tbsp olive oil
¼ cup white vinegar
½ cup lemon juice (from a real lemon)
2 Tbsp raw honey
2 tsp black pepper
2 cloves garlic, finely minced

Set aside the raw honey in advance, in order for it to melt (setting it in a pan of hot water can speed up the process). Mix all ingredients in a small bowl to completely dissolve the honey. Store any unused marinade in an airtight container in the refrigerator up to 2 weeks. Make about 1 cup. ❶

Lemon & Herb Marinade

1 cup of lemon juice (from a real lemon)
2 Tbsp olive oil
⅓ cup red wine vinegar
1 tsp dried oregano
1 tsp dried thyme
1 tsp black pepper
½ tsp sea salt
1 clove garlic, finely chopped

Combine all of the ingredients in a bowl, and mix well. ❶

Step right up!

Step right up, Step right up! Boy do I have a product for you!
It will do amazing things, I mean it is amazing, you've got to try it!
It will help you lose weight,
It will help you sleep better,
It will boost your high-density lipoprotein (HDL),
It will decrease unhealthy triglycerides,
It has been known to decrease your risk of Cardiovascular disease,
It will help a wide range of health problems and concerns including stroke, type 2 diabetes, and more...

Ladies and Gentlemen this product is amazing!

This product is...

EXERCISE!
30 minutes a day 5 times a week!

This is my favorite message from a doctor that I love, Dr. Ellie Campbell, DO.

When I first met Dr. Ellie Campbell, my friend, I heard her speak of taking care of your body; her message was understandable and clear. As soon as I heard her I decided to attend her seminar and learn more as she and I were speaking the same language. I encouraged some of my clients to attend her next seminar.

Dr. Campbell has her own medical practice in Forsyth County, GA.

To reach Dr. Campbell, DO, via internet:
www.campbellfamilymedicine.com
www.cfmradiantwellness.com

by mail:
Campbell Family Medicine
3925 Johns Creek Court Suite A
Suwanee GA 30024

For more information on an exercise plan please visit www.myhealthkick.com for a complimentary consultation.

Best Salsa Ever

1 15-oz can of tomato and pepper blend (mild flavor)
5-8 fresh organic tomatoes, diced
Juice of ½ lemon
¼ - ½ tsp of sea salt
½ Vidalia onion, chopped fine
Large bunch of cilantro (use ½ to all depending on the taste,
  start with ½) snipped fine without all of it's stems.

Toss together in a large bowl, let flavors mix 30 minutes or overnight before serving. Serve with dipping veggies or chips. If any left overs, eat within 2 days. It wilts quickly. ❶

Best Guacamole Ever

Mix equal portions of diced avocado with the salsa above. If necessary, add the juice of ½ lemon and ½ tsp sea salt.

Mix, taste, and enjoy! ❶

ABOUT THE AUTHOR

Wendy Hood is a mother of three, Tyler, Tori, and Taryn, and is a wife to Dennis. She and her husband work together at My H.E.A.L.T.H. Kick™, and The Swing Doctor. Dennis' expertise is with the baseball players. He coaches two baseball teams and specializes in hitting instruction. More information about Dennis at www.baseballswingdoctor.com

Wendy teaches Kickboxing, P.E. classes, Martial Arts, and also works with clients on Personal Training. One of Wendy's passions is to help individuals reach their health goals. She does this through fitness plans, providing healthy recipes and menus, and being her clients accountability partner until the goal is reached. My H.E.A.L.T.H. Kick™ was formed in 2005.

Wendy works with clients via phone or in person and helps them achieve their health goals.

You may contact the author by internet:
www.myhealthkick.com

or by mail:
1195 Samples Industrial Drive
Cumming, GA 30041

Recipe Index

Breakfast

Salads

Wraps

Sides & Pastas

Beef

Chicken & Turkey

Notes